# ARE YOU THERE GOD?
# IT'S ME, MARGARET.

*Judy Blume*

AUTHORED by Kathryn Gundersen
UPDATED AND REVISED by Patrick Kennedy

COVER DESIGN by Table XI Partners LLC
COVER PHOTO by Olivia Verma and © 2005 GradeSaver, LLC

BOOK DESIGN by Table XI Partners LLC

Published by GradeSaver LLC, www.gradesaver.com

First published in the United States of America by GradeSaver LLC. 2014

GRADESAVER, the GradeSaver logo and the phrase "Getting you the grade
since 1999" are registered trademarks of GradeSaver, LLC

ISBN 978-1-60259-435-7

Printed in the United States of America

For other products and additional information please visit
http://www.gradesaver.com

# Table of Contents

# Table of Contents

# Biography of Blume, Judy (1938-)

Judy Blume was born to Esther and Ralph Sussman and raised in Elizabeth, New Jersey. She has an older brother, David, and her family is Jewish. In 1956, Blume graduated from Battin High School, then moved on to attend Boston University. During her first semester, however, she contracted mononucleosis and took some time off from school, before finishing college at New York University and obtaining a bachelor's degree in teaching.

She married John Blume, a future lawyer, in the summer of her sophomore year of college. The Blumes had two children: Randy Lee, who became an airline pilot, and Lawrence Andrew, who became a filmmaker. However, in 1975 the couple separated, though Blume still kept her former husband's last name. Shortly after, she married a physicist named Thomas A. Kitchens, but they separated only two years later. Finally, in 1987 she married George Cooper, who had a daughter Amanda from a previous marriage. Blume and Cooper now live in Key West.

Since Blume had been an avid reader since childhood, her choice of a writing career seemed natural. She first started writing when her children were in preschool, and her first published book was titled *The One in the Middle is the Green Kangaroo*. In the decade that followed, she published 13 more books aimed at young adults. After creating these narratives, Blume began to tackle the adult genre and wrote numerous bestsellers including *Wifey*. Blume has won more than 90 literary awards, including three U.S. lifetime achievement awards.

# About Are You There God? It's Me, Margaret.

*Are you there God? It's Me, Margaret*, one of Judy Blume's most successful young adult novels, was published in 1970. The book appeared only shortly after Blume began her literary career, while her young children were still in preschool. *Are you there God? It's Me, Margaret* has been praised for its exploration of important adolescent themes, including puberty, menstruation, and crushes, not to mention more serious topics such as choosing a single religion to live by. It was one of the first novels of its time to touch upon these subjects, and was widely read both by young adults growing up around its publication and by members of the following generations.

Blume has said that she felt like she'd always known the protagonist, Margaret, even before sitting down to write her story. When Blume was in sixth grade herself, she dealt with many of the same concerns that confronted Margaret—developing physically like the other girls, wearing a bra, and getting her period. Just like Margaret, she had a very personal relationship with God, regardless of organized religion. At the same time, though, Margaret's family is very different from Blume's own; this novel's narrative, while based in reality, is very much a product of the imagination. Blume has said that Margaret's story brought her her first and most loyal readers.

*Are You There God? It's Me, Margaret* has won numerous literary awards. Upon its publication in 1970, it was named a *New York Times* Outstanding Book of the Year. In 2005, it was placed on *Time* Magazine's All-Time 100 Novels list, and in 2011, it was placed on the same publication's Top 100 fiction books written in English since 1923 list. The novel's success inspired Blume to write a companion book, *Then Again, Maybe I Won't*, which tells a similar story from a boy's perspective, though the secondary themes in this juvenile novel are considerably different.

About Are You There God? It's Me, Margaret.

# Character List

**Margaret Simon**

Margaret is the eleven-year-old protagonist of Blume's novel and has just moved from New York City to Farbrook, New Jersey. She's extremely concerned with growing up, getting her period, wearing a bra, and liking boys. Since Margaret's parents practice separate religions, Margaret has no religion of her own and is expected to decide for herself what faith she wants to follow when she gets older.

**Barbara Simon**

Margaret's mother and a former practicing Christian, Barbara passes her time by creating still life paintings. Barbara's parents stopped speaking to her once she married Margaret's father, who is Jewish.

**Herb Simon**

Herb is Margaret's father, and is of Jewish descent. Upon moving out to Farbrook, he began to commute to his job in New York City.

**Sylvia Simon**

A proud New Yorker, Sylvia is Margaret's paternal grandmother. Sylvia is extremely doting and loves to spoil Margaret, which makes Margaret's parents uneasy; in fact, Sylvia was part of the reason why Margaret's family left New York in the first place. Sylvia is committed to her Jewish faith and hopes that Margaret will choose to follow the same religion.

**Nancy Wheeler**

As Margaret's best friend in her new town, Nancy was the first one to reach out and invite Margaret over. Nancy is very proud and feels that she knows a lot about issues such as boys, bras, and periods, and likes to flaunt this knowledge when in the company of her friends.

**Gretchen Potter**

One of Margaret's close friends in her new town, Gretchen is also the daughter of the doctor Margaret's father visits following an accident with a new lawnmower.

**Janie Loomis**

One of Margaret's close friends in her new town, Janie is one of the shyer sixth-graders, yet Margaret is able to bond with her easily.

**Evan Wheeler**

Evan is Nancy's older brother, who is girl-obsessed and often spies on the PTS group.

## Moose Freed

Evan Wheeler's best friend, Moose cuts grass for the families in the neighborhood, including the Simons. Margaret has a secret crush on Moose throughout the entire novel.

## Mr. Benedict

Mr. Benedict is the new, relatively young sixth grade teacher. At the beginning of the year, the students give him a lot of trouble, yet Mr. Benedict soon finds ways to quietly earn the obedience of the class.

## Philip Leroy

Philip is a handsome boy in the sixth grade, the one who ranks at the top in all four PTS Boy Books. Despite his appealing looks, Philip is actually rather immature.

## Jay Hassler

A boy who ranks near the top in Margaret's Boy Book, Jay is polite and has nice eyes.

## Laura Danker

Laura is a girl in the sixth grade who is significantly more developed, physically, than all the other girls and is the subject of vicious rumors because of her early maturation.

## Norman Fishbein

Norman is a boy in the sixth grade; Margaret calls him a "drip," but her opinion of him increases somewhat when he throws a dinner party for everyone in the class.

## Mr. Hutchins

Margaret's maternal grandfather, Mr. Hutchins is extremely Christian and disowned his daughter when she chose a Jewish husband.

## Mrs. Hutchins

Margaret's maternal grandmother, Mrs. Hutchins shares her husband's firm devotion to Christianity.

## Mrs. Wheeler

Nancy's mother, Mrs. Wheeler is extremely involved in the neighborhood social scene and the school PTA.

# Major Themes

### Coming-of-Age

The literary term for a novel such as *Are You There God? It's Me, Margaret* is *bildungsroman*, or coming-of-age story. Throughout the course of the school year described in this novel, Margaret truly does come of age, transitioning from a young girl to a young woman and learning much in the process about her desires, her companions, and the way the world works. Margaret hits many milestones in the course of her journey—her first crush, her first bra, her first kiss, her first period—and at the end, she ceases to constantly wish she were someone else and learns to be satisfied in her own skin.

### Religion

Religion plays an important role in Margaret's life, but not in the manner that many readers might expect: rather than adhering to formal religious principles, Margaret *doesn't* have a set faith. Throughout the novel, she tries desperately to discover where she fits—Judaism or Christianity—and deals repeatedly with the pressures and biases of the adults around her. But Margaret's true connection to religion comes not when she sits in a mass or at temple, but when she is alone and talks to God on her own. In such private conditions, she truly feels a sense of religious devotion.

### Conformity

A huge part of adolescence is the pressure to conform, and Margaret feels that pressure more strongly than ever after she moves to New Jersey. As the new girl in her public school, she tries extremely hard to fit in and find her place, and as a result of peer pressure does some things she might not normally do; for instance, she helps to "initiate" the new teacher, Mr. Benedict, with tricks and pranks. She also feels the pressure to conform in religious matters; because it isn't normal for a girl her age not to have a faith, she feels that she needs to select one as soon as possible in order to be like everyone else.

### Friendship

The very first person to reach out and welcome Margaret to her new home—Nancy—becomes Margaret's best friend, and through her, Margaret makes other friends who are crucial to her development. Margaret's friends make her feel that she belongs, and she regards their offered advice and wisdom with great seriousness. Her friendship with Nancy is tested when she learns that Nancy lied about getting her period, but Margaret realizes that their bond is more important than holding a grudge. In Blume's narrative, friendship is a crucial component of growing up, and Margaret would not have confronted the challenges of adolescence quite as easily without her friends by her side.

## Family

Though Margaret's family situation is in many ways a subplot, Margaret's parents and grandparents still play important roles in her development. Margaret's family structure is a bit unusual for her time; she has two loving parents, yes, but no siblings and only one grandmother who speaks to her (and who can sometimes be a little too doting). The Simons' family bonds are tested when her Margaret's distant maternal grandparents come to visit, and this meeting certainly does not end with a happy reconciliation. In the end, however, Margaret realizes that the people who are truly important are always ready to provide her with all the love and affection she needs.

## Adolescence

*Are You There God? It's Me, Margaret* explores the trials and tribulations of that turbulent period called adolescence. During this stage in life, puberty takes control, and hormones and emotions run rampant as young people try to cope with growing up physically and trying to fit in socially all at the same time. Adolescence is certainly a struggle for Margaret, who feels that she is behind her peers in many ways, but she handles it the best she can. While Margaret's adolescent stage doesn't come to a conclusion in the novel, Margaret does seem to have a better grasp of her own identity by the final chapter.

## Rumors

Children can be verbally vicious, and this fact is most prominently exemplified through the character of Laura Danker. Laura has not actually done anything to merit the other students' shoddy treatment of her; she has simply grown and developed more quickly than they have, yet as a result, the other children her age spread rumors that Laura is sexually active. Much of this gossip is motivated by jealousy, at least on the part of the sixth-grade girls. Yet in the end, Margaret realizes how powerful rumors can be and comes to understand that she shouldn't believe everything she hears; it's much better to get to know someone in depth, and in person, before forming judgments.

# Glossary of Terms

**A&P**
a supermarket chain.

**bust**
a woman's chest.

**cufflink**
a device for fastening together the sides of a shirt cuff.

**delicatessen**
the long word for "deli."

**elope**
to run away secretly in order to get married.

**expel**
to kick out of school.

**Good Yom Tov**
Happy New Year (Hebrew).

**hymn**
a religious song written for the purpose of praise or adoration.

**Lincoln Center**
a performing arts complex in midtown Manhattan, New York.

**lingerie**
women's underwear and nightclothes.

**loafers**
a leather shoe shaped like a moccasin with a low heel.

**mensturation**
a girl or woman's monthly period.

**pageant**
a procession or performance, often involving elaborate costumes.

**Playboy**

A men's magazine famous for its pictures of nude women.

**PTS**

Pre-Teen Sensations; the name for the secret club created by Margaret and her friends.

**rabbi**

a Jewish religious teacher.

**Rosh Hashanah**

Jewish new-year.

**sermon**

a speech about a moral or religious subject, normally delivered during a service.

**The Y**

The YMCA, or Young Man's Christian Association.

**yarmulke**

a small, round Jewish headpiece.

# Short Summary

Margaret Simon, eleven years-old, has lived her entire life in New York City. Yet one day her parents decide to move out to the small suburb of Farbrook, New Jersey. Margaret suspects that her parents want to get her away from her father's mother, Sylvia, who pampers her. For her own part, Margaret is about to enter the sixth grade at a brand new school, and much like the typical adolescent girl of her age, she begins to worry about issues such as boys, bras, and periods. She often speaks to God about these things, but privately—she has her own personal connection to God yet does not follow a formal religion.

After making friends with three other girls her age—Nancy Wheeler, Gretchen Potter, and Janie Loomis—Margaret joins their secret club, the Pre-Teen Sensations (PTSes) in order to discuss topics such as boys and puberty, and to experience the thrill of growing up at last. Over the course of her sixth-grade year, Margaret reaches many milestones, notably getting her first bra and having her first kiss with the handsomest boy in the class, Philip Leroy, during a game at a class dinner party.

But Margaret has additional concerns, ones that other children her age typically aren't forced to deal with. Because Margaret's mother is Christian and her father is Jewish, Margaret was not raised in a particular religion, and instead her parents told her she could choose a religion for herself once she was old enough. When Margaret's sixth-grade teacher, Mr. Benedict, assigns each student an individual yearlong project, Margaret decides to do hers on religion, and accompanies her grandmother to temple and two of her friends to church in her attempts to understand different faiths. To her dismay, though, she can't feel her connection to God in the context of any formal religion; it's only when she's alone, talking to God, that she feels a divine presence.

Margaret is tested even more when, towards the end of the novel, her maternal grandparents visit for the first time. (As devout Christians, they had refused to speak to Margaret's mother after she married a Jewish man.) Since these grandparents ruin Margaret's plans to visit Sylvia in Florida, Margaret is determined not to like them—and she doesn't, especially when they try to insist that Margaret was born a Christian girl. By the end of the school year, Margaret has reached a stalemate on religion; she has decided that she still isn't ready to choose a faith. The novel ends with Margaret getting her first period at last and realizing that, when she's patient, the things she wants will always come.

# Quotes and Analysis

*"Are You There, God? It's Me, Margaret."*

*Margaret - Throughout*

The title phrase of Blume's book is repeated every time Margaret speaks to God privately, often reporting events of her day or asking for something she desperately wants. These words also illustrate Margaret's unique connection to God; even though she doesn't practice a religion, she still feels God's presence and, arguably, relies on God as much as someone who follows a formal religion would.

*"My mother says Grandma is too much of an influence on me."*

*Margaret - Chapter 1, pg 2*

This is one of the first quotes that characterizes the doting, slightly overbearing Sylvia Simon. Sylvia certainly is a handful, and it is understandable that Margaret's parents would want to keep their daughter beyond Sylvia's extreme influence. At the same time, since Margaret's other grandparents do not talk to Margaret or her parents, Sylvia's presence in her life is often constructive and reassuring. It's clear that Margaret loves her grandmother very much, and the two share the kind of close familial bond that Margaret doesn't form with too many other people.

*"Nancy says nobody in the sixth grade wears socks on the first day of school!"*

*Margaret - Chapter 4, pg 24*

This quotation, which is taken from a passing argument between Margaret and her mother, accurately displays the pressure Margaret feels to conform to her peers. Though this pressure is present for everyone her age, Margaret's status as the new girl in a new school accentuates it even more. Throughout her story, Margaret does many things that she wouldn't choose to do on her own, sometimes because she simply believes that everyone around her does the same and that it is necessary to fit in.

*"I like long hair, tuna fish, the smell of rain and things that are pink. I hate pimples, baked potatoes, when my mother's mad, and religious holidays."*

*Margaret - Chapter 4, pg 27-28*

This quote, referenced on the jackets of some editions of the novel and offered directly in Chapter 4, comes from Margaret's response to the "About Me" assignment, which Mr. Benedict gives his sixth-grade students on their first day of school. These sentences characterize Margaret in two ways: first, as a typical adolescent girl, who likes long hair and pink things and hates pimples; second, as someone with a few deeper struggles in her young life, particularly where religion is concerned. Margaret is a complex and very real character, and we can learn a lot about her from these two simple sentences.

*"Well, you're really growing up, Margaret. No more little girl."*

*Mr. Simon - Chapter 7, pg 44*

Margaret's father says this to Margaret after she buys her first bra, but this quote sums up the coming-of-age theme of the entire novel. Margaret is bridging the sometimes awkward gap between being little girl and being a young woman, and her actions over the course of the story often serve to ease this strange transition in whatever ways possible. Blume chose to explore growing up and puberty precisely because these topics were relatively neglected by novelists during the early 1970s, even though all girls experience these important stages at some point.

*"We must, we must, we must increase our bust!"*

*Nancy - Chapter 7, pg 46*

This is the chant that Nancy tells her fellow Pre-Teen Sensations to repeat, while performing stretching exercises, in order to grow their chests enough to fill out their bras and truly become women. These words are representative of Nancy's self-proclaimed vast knowledge of what it means to go through puberty and grow up; Nancy always appears to be so sure of herself. At moments, however, Nancy's confidence seems to crack, particularly when Margaret finds out that Nancy was lying about having her period.

*"It's not so much that I like him as a person God, but as a boy he's very handsome."*

*Margaret - Chapter 10, pg 65*

This quote, part of Margaret's speech to God just before the class square dance, represents the attitude that Margaret and her friends have toward boys. They believe that certain boys are made to be liked simply on account of good looks; even though Philip Leroy (the "handsome" boy of the quotation) can be an immature jerk, Margaret and her friends still all keep him as the top boy in their Boy Books. And Margaret is determined to be Philip's partner at the square dance. For girls of this age, there is a lot of pressure to start having crushes, but in many ways the girls are too young to understand what such attachments really mean.

*"As long as she loves me and I love her, what difference does religion make?"*

*Margaret - Chapter 23, pg 141*

At the time of this quote, Margaret has experienced religious pressure not only from her maternal grandparents, but also from Sylvia. Even the efforts of her most beloved grandparent frustrate and upset Margaret. In Margaret's eyes, religion shouldn't matter. It shouldn't affect her relationship with her family and the people who love her, and by this point in the novel, Margaret is coming to realize that she shouldn't be forced to choose Judaism or Christianity in order to determine her identity.

*"You always believe everything you hear about other people?"*

*Moose - Chapter 25, pg 146*

Though he is an unlikely source of wisdom, Moose reminds Margaret of a very important lesson for an adolescent: you shouldn't always believe what you hear. Rumors can be vicious, and Margaret learns this the hard way when she takes her anger out on Laura Danker. It is wrong to judge a person based on what others say about him or her; as in the case of Laura, false rumors can be started out of hatred, jealousy, or even just a feeling of difference.

*"Thank you, God. Thanks an awful lot."*

*Margaret - Chapter 25, pg 149*

As is true of many quotations that end famous novels, these last words sum up the story of *Are You There God? It's Me, Margaret* in a poignant and powerful way. For the few weeks leading up to this point, Margaret has been rejecting God despite the bond she once felt with him, believing that he is allowing bad things into her life. Now, though, she realizes that if she's patient, good things will happen to her—it just takes time for these things to come. With this in mind, Margaret rekindles her personal relationship with God and continues to talk to him, presumably well beyond the ending of the novel.

# Summary and Analysis of Chapters 1-3

Margaret Simon, who is 11 years old, has always lived in an apartment with her family in New York City. Now, though, her family is moving to the New York area suburb of Farbrook, New Jersey, where Margaret's dad can still commute to Manhattan for work and where Margaret's mom can have all the "grass, trees, and flowers she ever wanted."

Margaret thinks that her parents left the city because her paternal grandmother, Sylvia Simon, has had too much of an influence on her. As an only child, Margaret has always been quite spoiled by her grandmother. Since Sylvia doesn't like public transportation and doesn't own a car, Margaret guesses she won't be seeing much of her doting grandparent.

Soon after the Simons move in, a neighbor Margaret's age, Nancy Wheeler, comes to visit their new house and invites Margaret over to play in the sprinklers. Margaret can't find her bathing suit and borrows one of Nancy's, but she's embarrassed to change in front of Nancy because her chest hasn't begun to grow yet. She feels underdeveloped and self-conscious, until Nancy asks Margaret if she's ever kissed a boy and admits that she hasn't. Nancy is obsessed with growing up, and keeps a drawer full of makeup that she intends to wear in public in the future, but simply tests out for the time being.

Margaret then meets Nancy's mother, who hopes that Margaret's mother will be active in local organizations, including a carpool to Sunday School. Margaret, however, doesn't attend Sunday school; since her mother is Christian and her father is Jewish, Margaret has not been raised with a particular religion, and is instead expected to choose her own once she's old enough. The two girls go outside to run around in the sprinklers, but Nancy's older brother Evan turns the water on full blast, drenching Margaret and Nancy. Margaret also meets Evan's friend Moose, who offers to cut the Simons' lawn.

Later that night, Margaret talks to God about her new home. Though she isn't formally religious, she has a very personal relationship with God and often talks to God when she's alone.

Determined to do his own yardwork, Margaret's father initially turns down Moose's offer, but after an awful accident with a new lawnmower, he decides to give the work to Moose after all. It also turns out that the doctor who treats the injured Mr. Simon has a daughter Margaret's age. Then, the day before school starts, Margaret's grandma suddenly appears at the house in New Jersey, laden down with food for Labor Day. Margaret's parents aren't especially thrilled with this appearance; for her part, Sylvia tells Margaret that they'll still be as close as ever, even though Margaret has moved away from the city.

# Analysis

These first three chapters serve primarily to introduce us to Margaret's life and to set up the essential background information for her later adventures. The setting—the suburb of Farbrook, New Jersey—is efficiently established. Many of the major characters, including the members of Margaret's family and Margaret's new neighbors, are revealed, and we gain insight into their lives and personalities based on how they act in these few chapters. We learn that Nancy tries to be sophisticated and grown-up, that her mother is very involved with life in the neighborhood, that Margaret's grandmother spoils her, and that Margaret's parents disapprove of Sylvia's constant involvement. Much is revealed through small conflicts and quick reactions.

Blume's decision to begin her story with these events seems especially natural, since Margaret *herself* is experiencing a beginning, too. We're not simply thrown into her world in the middle of great drama; her story opens as she moves to a new place, so we as readers are learning all about her new home and new surroundings as well. Margaret does not have to spend time explaining everything; new events unfold for us exactly as they unfold for Margaret. This is one of the many reasons why readers feel such a connection to Margaret: we can get inside her mind and share her brand-new experiences.

Although Blume's novel has not dwelled much on the subject of religion just yet, it is important to keep religions matters in mind as we read on. Even the basics will be important later: Margaret's mother is Christian, her father is Jewish, and yet she hasn't been raised in any religion at all. Her grandmother, who dotes on her and gives her huge helpings of attention, subtly pressures her towards Judaism.

Nonetheless, Margaret is supposed to decide for herself what she wants to be, if anything—it's a monumental decision, a lot to think about for someone who's just entering sixth grade. Remember the theme of religion while reading on, because (as both the title and these few chapters indicate) it will play a major role in the rest of this novel.

# Summary and Analysis of Chapters 4-6

Margaret is nervous as she prepares for her first day of school. Because Nancy told her that no one wears socks with loafers, Margaret decides not to wear socks; unfortunately, her feet are aching and blistered by the time she finishes walking to the school building. When she gets to school, though, she sees that some of the girls are wearing socks anyway.

The teacher for Margaret's sixth-grade class is new, since the previous teacher had left the year before; he comes in and immediately writes his name, "Miles J. Benedict, Jr.," on the board. He is young and attractive, and this is his very first teaching position. He asks all of his students to fill out "about me" questionnaires. Margaret does so, listing her likes, dislikes, and a few of her views on life. Yet Margaret also has social issues to consider. During the day, Nancy slips Margaret a note telling her that the secret club will meet that day after school.

The other girls in the secret club, which convenes at Nancy's house, are Janie Loomis and Gretchen Potter. Nancy and the other Farbrook girls immediately begin gossiping about a girl named Laura Danker, who is more developed than the rest of the girls and has a bad reputation for "going behind the A&P" with boys. Janie is also convinced that Laura has already had her period, and it is revealed that none of the other girls have had it yet, which makes Margaret feel relieved about her own lack of development.

The girls then begin trying to think of a club name; after trying a few different options, they decide on the Four PTSes (Pre-Teen Sensations) and give each other code names. Nancy is Alexandra, and Margaret is Mavis.

After swearing an oath of secrecy, each of the four girls is required to think up a rule for the new club. Nancy's rule is that all members must wear bras, which makes both Margaret and Janie uncomfortable because they haven't started wearing bras yet. Gretchen declares that the first one to get her period has to tell the others all about it. Nancy says they all need to keep a Boy Book, which is a list of boys in order of preference. Unable to think of a better rule, Margaret decides that the PTSes should meet on a certain day each week. When Gretchen declares she can't do Tuesdays or Thursdays because of Hebrew School, the discussion turns to Margaret's lack of religion.

After some prompting, Margaret tells the story behind her unusual status: her maternal grandparents in Ohio refused to accept a Jewish son-in-law. On her end, Sylvia wasn't particularly happy about having a Christian daughter-in-law, but she accepted the situation. The other girls seem most interested in the social side of all this; they wonder aloud how Margaret's family is going to decide between a membership at the Y and the Jewish Community Center. Eventually, the newly-created PTSes decide that they will meet on Mondays, and Margaret goes home and informs her mother that she would like to begin wearing a bra.

At school the next day, Mr. Benedict asks Margaret why she wrote on her questionnaire that she hates religious holidays. She doesn't want to tell him at first, but finally she admits that her parents don't adhere to any particular religion and neither does she, though she is supposed to choose one when she grows up.

Later, Sylvia calls and tells Margaret she's arranged for them to get tickets for Lincoln Center shows one Saturday every month. Luckily, the Lincoln Center outings won't be starting right away, because that Saturday Margaret and her mother are going bra shopping. During this shopping trip, Margaret chooses a special bra called a Gro-Bra, which will grow with her as her bust expands. While paying, Margaret runs into Janie, who is shopping for a bra of her own.

## Analysis

It is becoming clear that Margaret's move represents so much more than just a switch of homes, towns, and schools. In a rather sudden fashion, Margaret has begun to realize that she is growing up, and it is becoming pretty clear that she's still a bit uncomfortable with this process. The friends Margaret is surrounded with have a lot to do with it; apparently, they've been thinking and talking for a while now about all the changes they're about to go through, while Margaret is only just being confronted with some of these new ideas. Yet her three new friends could also facilitate her growth over the course of the novel.

Another major part of the setting is introduced in these chapters: Margaret's new school. A lot of the novel will undoubtedly take place here, and much of the pressure she feels to grow up faster will come from the environment and the people Margaret encounters in sixth grade. Since all of the girls in the sixth grade are experiencing puberty at different rates, the differences between them can arouse feelings of being out of place, or even inspire vicious rumors, as evidenced by Laura Danker. The interactions that take place at Margaret's school are meant to teach Blume's readers important lessons about accepting differences, particularly during adolescence.

Another character with an uneasy place at the school, Mr. Benedict, is introduced in these chapters as well. Just like Margaret, Mr. Benedict is almost entirely new to Farbrook, and he must earn the respect of the students; the two characters, though fairly far apart in age, certainly parallel each other. And they can undoubtedly learn a lot from each other over the course of the novel.

There is another aspect of Mr. Benedict's situation that involves a degree of tension. Through the students' initial reactions to having a male teacher, it becomes pretty clear that Mr. Benedict's position was very unusual during this time period. (Remember, Blume's novel was written in 1970). Today, grammar school staffs are much more mixed in terms of gender; many students today wouldn't think twice about having a male teacher instead of a female teacher.

In these chapters, we also learn a little bit more about Margaret's religious situation and about the sources of her confusion in religious matters. Margaret has had very little exposure to either Judaism or Christianity, since her parents stopped practicing after they got married. The community around her is very religiously observant, so it seems that the topic has suddenly come up on her radar in a way that, perhaps, it never had before. This is a lot for Margaret to think about while she's facing the social and biological challenges of adolescence, but the constant discussions of the Y versus the Jewish Community Center, and Mr. Benedict's willingness to confront her about hating religious holidays, foreshadow greater religious issues to come.

# Summary and Analysis of Chapters 7-9

Margaret tries on her new bra as soon as she gets home, and her dad embarrasses her at the dinner table that night by congratulating her on growing up. That Monday in school, Margaret quickly examines the boys in her class to determine which ones she wants to add to her Boy Book for the PTS meeting later in the day.

Then, Mr. Benedict announces that each student must begin working on a yearlong project about an individually-selected topic that is meaningful or important. He is noticeably disappointed when the students don't seem particularly excited about this assignment. Margaret acknowledges that nobody in the class is particularly scared of Mr. Benedict, even though students should normally be a little scared of their teacher.

At the club meeting, it is revealed that all the members except for Nancy have purchased Gro-Bras rather than regularly-sized bras. The girls then examine their Boy Books, and it is revealed that every single girl in the club has named Philip Leroy as the number one most attractive boy. When the meeting ends, the four girls notice that Nancy's brother Evan and Evan's friend Moose have been eavesdropping.

The next day at school, the students cause trouble for Mr. Benedict by making "peep" noises over and over, but dispersed throughout the classroom so that Mr. Benedict can't pinpoint the culprit. The following morning, Mr. Benedict rearranges the students' desks in a "U" shape, and Margaret sits next to Laura Danker. This takes care of the peeping problem, but when the students take a social studies test, everyone in the class decides that nobody will put their names on the test, so that Mr. Benedict can't grade the papers.

To the students' surprise, though, the next morning all their names are on the proper test papers; Margaret had done extremely well. Mr. Benedict has been victorious in this second conflict with his class. Margaret herself begins to think about her year-long assignment again, and decides to perform a project based on religion and on her process of choosing a faith.

That Saturday, Margaret visits Lincoln Center with Sylvia for the first of their planned outings, and

tells her grandma she wants to go to temple with her to learn what being Jewish is all about. Obviously, Sylvia is thrilled, but Margaret's parents aren't too pleased when they are informed of this plan. Margaret accompanies her grandma to a service on Rosh Hashanah morning, and tries to get a feel for what temple is like. Afterwards, she meets the rabbi. She doesn't feel anything particularly special, but she's excited to be on the way to choosing a religion.

# Analysis

These few chapters deal in depth with the themes of conformity and peer pressure. In modern society, the pressure for adolescents to do what everyone else is doing in order to fit in is enormous, and Margaret clearly experiences a lot of this kind of pressure in her new school. Undoubtedly, a few kids in the sixth-grade class really do think it will be funny to play tricks on the new teacher; the others merely go along with the crowd, not wanting to be dissenters and acknowledging that if they're misbehaving in a large group, they can't all get in trouble. Conformity plays a huge role in the lives of these adolescents, as these chapters make evident.

The idea of "testing" the new teacher is something that many students today can relate to; whether dealing with a substitute, a leave replacement, or a new hire, we have all given our new teachers at least a *little* bit of trouble at one point or another. It's almost like an initiation; Mr. Benedict will have to earn the respect of his students. In a way, he's already begun to; he must certainly have spent a lot of time matching names to test papers, but he succeeds in commanding his students' attention and silencing their mischief. Judging by his character and his actions, Mr. Benedict is idealistic but not oblivious; though he has high hopes for his class, he will not let the kids walk all over him. Mr. Benedict and his special projects for the class will certainly prove to be interesting additions to this novel.

At last, Margaret has taken her first steps towards choosing a religion. Though using an exploration of religion as her project idea should be helpful to her in many ways, this project might also put unnecessary pressure on her to choose more quickly than she would have without it. An important question to address in this situation is whether Margaret herself wants to choose right away, or whether she simply feels the pressure to conform.

It certainly seems that social pressure plays a role in Margaret's approach to religion, since she constantly brings up the idea of joining the Y or the Jewish Community Center just like everyone else. It is to be hoped that, along the way, these motives will change as Margaret learns more and more about Christianity and Judaism. Perhaps she will be legitimately ready to choose a faith for her own reasons, or else she will realize that she does not have to choose right away and can instead focus on growing up, which for Margaret is undoubtedly a full-time job.

# Summary and Analysis of Chapters 10-12

Margaret goes to church for the first time with Janie Loomis, who is becoming one of Margaret's closest friends. Margaret observes that church is almost exactly like temple, except that the service is in English rather than in Hebrew; just as in temple, she counts the colorful hats in the rows in front of her. Janie introduces Margaret to the minister, and mentions that Margaret has no religion, which embarrasses Margaret. Later, Margaret speaks to God and apologizes for not feeling any sort of connection to God in church, and promises that she'll try harder next time.

Soon after this, the PTA announces that it will be hosting a Thanksgiving square dance for the sixth grade, and Nancy knows all about this event because her mother is on the organizing committee. For the square dance, all of the PTSes want to dance with Philip Leroy, the boy at the top of their Boy Books. For the next few weeks, the sixth-grade gym periods are devoted to square dancing lessons, and when Mr. Benedict needs to demonstrate steps, he uses the tall Laura Danker as his partner. This choice makes the PTSes exchange looks.

Then the dance itself arrives. The gym is decorated, the organizing adults wear costumes, and the class has an actual square dance caller to lead the event along. After some dancing, at last Margaret gets to dance with Philip Leroy, but he keeps stepping on her feet.

By December, the PTSes stop using their secret code names, which are too confusing, and abandon their Boy Books, since the names never change. Margaret wonders if they all put Philip Leroy simply because he's handsome and because the PTSes are all afraid to acknowledge which boys they really like. For one of the girls' meetings, Gretchen manages to steal her father's anatomy book, and the girls look at pictures of bodies, particularly male ones. Margaret also sneaks in one of her father's copies of *Playboy* magazine because the girls have never seen one, and as they look at it, they all wish they could grow up to look like the nude woman in the centerfold photo.

In the middle of December, Margaret's grandma goes on her annual three-week Caribbean cruise, and the family gives her a bon voyage party in her room on the ship. Margaret's mother then begins sending out holiday cards. Of course, the Simons don't really celebrate Christmas; they give presents, because it's an American custom, but they never celebrate the way people who belong to a set religion do. Yet Margaret discovers that her mother is sending Christmas cards to Margaret's maternal grandparents, who disapprove of their daughter's marriage and never speak to Margaret or her parents.

At school, Mr. Benedict's class prepares to serve as the choir in the annual Christmas-Hanukkah pageant. They practice singing five different Christmas carols and three Hanukkah songs, as well as marching with partners—a boy named Norman

Fishbein ends up as Margaret's, and Margaret isn't at all thrilled by this circumstance. A week before the pageant, there's a bit of drama; a Jewish boy refuses to sing the Christmas songs because doing so is apparently against his religion, and a Christian girl refuses to sing the Hanukkah songs because doing so would be against hers. Aside from these objections, the pageant goes fairly smoothly.

## Analysis

As the holiday season approaches, Blume's chapters focus more and more on Margaret's religion dilemma. Margaret is disappointed by the lack of a special feeling she experiences when she visits church with Janie, and she is also confused by the fact that it's almost exactly like temple. The latter is an important point, and an important lesson in this novel—though different branches of religion may have different names and appear to be different, they are, in reality, all quite similar and meant for the same purpose. Margaret has been trying extremely hard to differentiate between Judaism and Christianity so that she can choose which she prefers, but the two faiths are a lot more similar than she could have predicted.

The small passages in which Margaret speaks to God are key components of this novel. Though Margaret does not yet belong to a religion, she still prays in her own personal way, and feels her own connection to God. It's fairly obvious that this connection is much stronger when she's alone and talking to him than when she's sitting in a congregation and trying to fit in, but she still feels pressured by the society around her (including her own beloved grandmother) to make a choice. If Margaret can realize that this connection she feels to God when she's alone is a form of genuine and rewarding faith, she might finally decide that she doesn't need to choose a religion right away.

It's interesting to note that despite the era when Blume's novel appeared—over 40 years ago—Margaret and her friends still behave almost exactly like many adolescent girls in the present day. This novel's depiction of preteens is truly universal. Just like today, the girls are always wishing to be something they are not yet or to have something they do not have—they want to grow up, they want their bodies to mature, they want their periods, they want Philip Leroy to like them. This is part of what makes this book so easy to relate to; all girls, at one point in their lives, have felt the way that Margaret and her friends do.

As Margaret settles into her new life, she begins to think more and more about boys. The girls study the male anatomy, discuss the boys in their class, and dream of becoming more appealing to them. But the point Margaret makes about the Boy Books is an important one, and shows her heightened awareness of the way she and her friends are behaving—Philip Leroy is probably only at the top of their books because he's handsome, and not because they particularly like him as a person. In a way, they are ashamed to admit which boys they *really* like; they have not yet reached the point where they are comfortable with their own feelings, because those feelings may not conform to the feelings of everyone else.

# Summary and Analysis of Chapters 13-15

After the holiday vacation begins, Margaret receives an invitation in the mail for Norman Fishbein's party. A few minutes later Nancy calls, and confirms that the entire class is invited to the party. The girls take this new event very seriously, and plan to wear their best party clothes. Margaret's opinion of Norman improves drastically as she gets excited about the party. While preparing, she takes a moment to look at herself naked in the mirror, and she asks God to help her grow more because she still feels like a little girl. Finally, she decides to stuff a few cotton balls into her bra to make her chest look bigger.

At the party, Nancy introduces Margaret to Norman's mother, and the girls then go to the basement with everyone else. Most of the class is there. For the most part, the boys and girls remain separated on opposite sides of the room. Everyone behaves very well until some of the boys decide to blow mustard through straws at the ceiling, which annoys Mrs. Fishbein. Nancy and another boy, Freddy Barnett, also get into a small fight when Freddy makes fun of the girls, and he ends up tearing the pocket off Nancy's dress. When she learns of this altercation, Mrs. Fishbein gets even more aggravated and threatens to send all the students home, but after she walks back upstairs the kids simply laugh at her.

Norman then announces that it's time to play games, and the first game he suggests is Guess Who: in this game, the lights must be turned off and the boys must guess which girl is which based on the way the girls feel above the neck. The girls will absolutely not have this, however, so the class begins playing Spin the Bottle. Norman spins Janie and kisses her on the cheek, and Janie does the same for Jay Hassler but first misses his face. Gretchen gets Philip Leroy, who then gets Laura Danker.

After this, the students start playing Two Minutes in the Closet, and Norman calls Gretchen's number first; they return long before their two minutes are through. Freddy then calls Laura, and Laura calls Philip. Then, to Margaret's surprise, Philip calls her. He actually kisses her on the mouth twice, though the kisses are really fast. Margaret is in such a daze afterward that she accidentally calls Norman's number, but tells him to kiss her fast on the cheek. Later that night, when Nancy tells Margaret she's probably the luckiest girl in the world, Margaret gloats by saying that Philip kissed her five times or so.

On Christmas Eve, Margaret goes to church with the Wheelers—afterward, she comes home and talks to God, saying she still hasn't felt any sort of connection during public worship. She asks him to give her a hint about which faith she should choose. Margaret's family situation, however, is changing quickly. When Sylvia returns from her cruise, she moves to Florida, declaring that New York has nothing to offer since Margaret is gone.

When school begins again, the girls see a movie about menstruation in their gym class, and only a week later, Gretchen is the first of the PTS girls to get her period. She tells the girls everything she can about what it felt like and what she did. Margaret frets about not getting hers yet, and begs God to let her get it soon. When Nancy is on vacation, Margaret gets a postcard from Nancy saying she's gotten her period too, and Margaret gets even more upset.

# Analysis

The party described in these chapters is a very symbolic event for Margaret and her classmates; it's their first taste of the sophisticated adult world, where they have to present themselves as respectable, grown-up individuals rather than as misbehaving children. It is clear that they take the preparations for this occasion quite seriously: all the girls wear their best dresses and are extremely polite to Mrs. Fishbein. However, once the party begins, this sophistication is compromised by moments of obvious immaturity. They students blow mustard at the ceiling, fight, and make fun of each other. Overall, the dinner party is a good starting experience, but events show that the sixth-graders haven't quite grown up yet—after all, becoming mature take time.

At the party, Margaret passes an important milestone on the road to growing up: she has her first kiss. Of course, it's merely a peck and it's received while playing a game, so this kiss doesn't necessarily represent mutual feelings. Yet for a girl who is extremely concerned with falling behind her peers, this new development serves as a huge confidence boost. Philip Leroy, the boy at the top of all four of the PTS Boy Books, voluntarily kisses Margaret on the mouth; just like buying a bra for the first time, this is an important step that makes Margaret feel good about her progress.

Unfortunately, though, this high isn't fated to last. Shortly after Norman Fishbein's party, two of Margaret's friends get their first periods and Margaret feels far behind once again. The novel is filled with shifts and reversals such as this: one moment, Margaret experiences something that makes her feel grown-up, and the next moment she's reminded once again that she's still a child. The transition from childhood to adulthood is never smooth, and this frustrates Blume's young protagonist to no end. It doesn't help that Margaret constantly feels as though she needs to compare herself to everyone around her; this puts even more pressure on her to accomplish things that are far beyond her control.

# Summary and Analysis of Chapters 16-18

Margaret goes to Lincoln Center twice with her mother, but this isn't as much fun as her earlier Lincoln Center outing with her grandmother. She writes Sylvia a letter filling her in on aspects of her life, and Sylvia writes back, mentioning a man she has met in Florida, Mr. Binamin. She wants Margaret to come visit her over the spring vacation. Margaret writes back, saying that her parents will probably give her their permission, though it's too soon to make plans yet. Still, Margaret is extremely excited, having never been on a plane before. At the end of her letter, Margaret adds that two of her friends have gotten their periods already.

At the beginning of March, Nancy invites Margaret to spend the day in New York City with her family and with Moose, who has been Margaret's secret crush for some time now. They all go to Radio City Music Hall and then to the Steak Place for dinner. When Nancy and Margaret go to the bathroom, Nancy begins to cry and asks Margaret to go and get her mother, yet she won't tell Margaret what's wrong.

It is quickly revealed that Nancy is getting her period—however, it's her first time, and she lied before when she told Margaret and the other PTSes that she'd gotten it. Margaret feels angry, but Nancy begs her not to tell, and says she thought she had had it before but had made a mistake. Margaret finally agrees, though she still feels betrayed by Nancy's lie. At the end of the chapter, Margaret speaks to God about what has happened, declaring that she won't lie and that she'll wait for a heavenly sign that she's ready to grow up.

Margaret turns twelve on March eighth, and the first thing she does is use her mom's deodorant because she thinks that, as a twelve-year-old, she's going to start having an odor under her arms. Her mom laughs and says that Margaret can buy deodorant of her own. Sylvia sends Margaret a savings bond and three handmade sweaters, as well as a round-trip airline ticket to Florida. In school, the class sings happy birthday to Margaret, the PTSes buy her a record as a gift, and Nancy mails Margaret a separate card thanking her for being a good best friend, which makes Margaret suspect that Nancy is still afraid her small lie will be revealed.

Soon, Mr. Benedict assigns his class a group project to work on, and Margaret is put in a group with Laura Danker, Philip Leroy, and Norman Fishbein. Philip Leroy is rude, and Margaret decides that she doesn't like him anymore; this makes Margaret upset with everyone and by the end of this group of chapters she has begun to complain that her birthday was horrible.

## Analysis

The scene with Nancy in New York City is certainly the most dramatic and revealing event that occurs in these chapters, and says a lot about Nancy's character as well. Of all the girls, Nancy has always been the leader. She flaunts her knowledge of worldly subjects and been the PTS spokesperson, while the rest follow along willingly. But here, for the first time, Nancy shows her true vulnerability. She's so concerned with growing up, so concerned with being the first to experience new sensations and pass along her knowledge to her friends, that she feels like she has to lie in order to maintain her persona. It's hard not to sympathize with Nancy, despite her lie; she is simply far too eager to grow up, and she doesn't mean any harm.

Margaret's reaction to Nancy's lie is also quite important. Nancy was Margaret's very first friend in New Jersey, the first person in a new town to reach out and talk to her. Margaret has always thought very highly of Nancy and held her in a positive light, since Nancy helped integrate her into her new life. It's natural that Margaret feels betrayed by the knowledge that Nancy is perhaps not as infallible and wise as was once thought, and it's also natural that Margaret feels hurt that her best friend lied about something so important. But her willingness to keep Nancy's secret says a lot about Margaret's character; she's upset, but she won't let that stop her from being a good friend all the same.

Now that Margaret has had her birthday and turned another year older, she will undoubtedly be even more impatient to feel like she's growing up. Though she's technically no different from who she was immediately before she turned twelve, her new label makes her feel older. With age comes maturity, or so she hopes. But everything that frustrates Margaret—her friend's lie, her lack of growth, her missed period, and the fact that boys like Philip Leroy are actually quite rude and immature—is slowly building up. Though her birthday itself wasn't horrible by any means, Margaret has accumulated enough pent-up frustration to convince herself that it was.

# Summary and Analysis of Chapter 19-21

The group project puts Margaret in a bad mood for three weeks. Philip Leroy is a bad worker, Norman works too slowly, and though Laura is a good worker, Margaret never tells her so because she's angry and jealous that the other girl has grown up so much faster than she has.

One day Laura makes a comment about needing to go to Confession at church, which makes Margaret wonder what Laura has to confess. Margaret picks a fight with Laura, and accuses her of going behind the A&P with boys. Laura is shocked and denies any such thing; she gets extremely upset and runs away, and Margaret begins to feel bad about what she did, realizing that the story about Laura's activities behind the A&P could be made up.

Margaret catches up with Laura to try to smooth things over, and Laura reveals that her size has always made her feel insecure. She says that she gets picked on because of it and she recounts how embarrassing it was to have to wear a bra in fourth grade and get called dirty names. Margaret apologizes, but Laura is still angry, and stalks off to Confession. Margaret feels like she has some things to confess, and follows; once inside the church, Margaret sits down at a booth and a voice behind a screen asks her to speak. She thinks it's God at first, then realizes it's only the priest. But the only words she can get out are "I'm sorry," and then she runs out of the church. That night, she tells God about the awful things she said to Laura and laments that she only feels God's presence when she's alone.

Just before spring break, a letter arrives. It is from Margaret's maternal grandparents, whom the Simons never speak to, and Margaret's father gets angry that Margaret's mother sent them a Christmas card. Margaret reads the letter herself; her grandparents say they that want to repair relations, and that they'll be flying out for a week to visit and meet Margaret. Margaret realizes that this means she can't go to Florida, and she gets extremely angry. Her mother calls Sylvia to tell her, and when Margaret is put on the phone she reveals to Sylvia that her other grandparents are coming to visit. Margaret is deeply upset, and she prays to God to make something happen so that these long-unseen grandparents won't visit, and so that she can go to Florida.

Both Margaret and her father are unhappy for the whole week leading up to the maternal grandparents' visit, but Margaret's mother asks everyone to understand that, while she hasn't forgiven her parents, she can't refuse to see them. When the Simons go to pick their guests up at the airport, Margaret's mother asks Margaret to understand that her grandparents did what they did to uphold their beliefs. The grandparents are excited to see the family, but Margaret begins to dislike these two relatives immediately. When they all go home, Margaret realizes that this visit is even harder on her father than it is on her.

The Simons and their guests try to make conversation over dinner, but the atmosphere is very tense. Margaret's father is asked about his job, then the talk turns to Margaret's uncle and his wife, and then to Margaret's schoolwork. Eventually, Margaret's grandparents ask how Margaret does in Sunday school; this is when a loaded conversation about religion starts. The two grandparents argue that Margaret has to have a religion, but her parents say that they're letting Margaret choose her own when she gets older. The grandparents argue back that a person must be born into a religion, and since you follow the religion of the mother, Margaret is Christian. Margaret gets up and storms out of the room, saying that she doesn't need a religion, nor does she need God.

## Analysis

A lot occurs in these three chapters, beginning with the Laura Danker incident. As has been explained previously, Margaret's pent-up frustration with her situation, coupled with the natural difficulties of working in almost any group, cause her to take out her annoyances on other people. In the process, she deeply hurts Laura Danker.

Laura's situation is a chilling example of the way children often treat other, perfectly innocent children who are simply different. Just because Laura has grown faster than all the other girls, she is the subject of vicious, hurtful rumors that alienate her from the rest of the class. The admirable thing about Laura, though, is that she never seems to seek revenge; she is quiet and helpful, and only reacts when Margaret confronts her in an extremely rude, even mean-spirited way.

As a result of this incident, Margaret has learned not to make judgments about people before she gets to know them; even more importantly, she's learned not to believe everything she hears about people from outside sources. It's clear that Margaret has never been exposed to many vicious rumors of this sort, since she doesn't know how to handle them; unfortunately, such rumors are a major part of adolescence, so it is unsurprising that gossip of this sort eventually reaches Margaret. In the end, she recognizes that she has made a mistake and apologizes; it can be hoped that Margaret has learned a lesson from this ordeal.

Margaret's experience in the Confession booth plays a pivotal role in her struggle to choose a defining religion. Margaret had acknowledged that she can't feel God's presence in the midst of a large, crowded church service, but this fact could be attributed to the number of people present. Perhaps aside from praying at home, Confession is the most private and personal component of religion, a context in which Margaret has a chance to admit her wrongdoings in the presence only of a priest and of God. But she still doesn't feel what she expects to feel, and in this moment, she realizes that attempting to force herself to feel close to a particular religion—whether Christianity or Judaism—isn't the best tactic.

The coercions of the people in her life don't make it any easier for Margaret to deal with religious questions, either. In light of Margaret's tense conflicts over growing up, making adult choices, and choosing a religion, her maternal grandparents' visit could not have come at a more inopportune time. Of course it is admirable that these relatives are trying to reconcile with the Simons, but clearly these grandparents still remain steadfast in their beliefs and do not understand Margaret's struggle. This is the final straw for the young girl; this visit pushes her to her breaking point, causing her to not only denounce organized religion, but to denounce God, to whom Margaret has always turned for comfort and guidance. She is denying an essential part of who she is because of the pressure she's been put under.

# Summary and Analysis of Chapters 22-25

Every time Margaret begins to talk to God, she now catches herself and stops. Desperate to get out of the house and away from her maternal grandparents, she has her mother drop her off downtown to see a movie with Janie. The two girls go into the drugstore first since they're early, and they decide to each buy a box of period pads, even though they're scared to do so. When Margaret gets home that day, she tries on one of the pads, and likes the way it feels. The next morning, Margaret's grandparents announce that they'll be going to stay at a hotel in New York instead of at the Simons' house, and Margaret is extremely upset because her grandparents ruined her vacation for nothing.

The next day the doorbell rings and, to Margaret's immense surprise, it's Sylvia. She's come up from Florida because Margaret couldn't come down, and she's brought her new beau, Mr. Binamin. They're both surprised to learn that Margaret's maternal grandparents have left already, and Sylvia asks if they tried any "church business." Margaret says yes, and Sylvia reminds her to never forget that she's a Jewish girl, which makes Margaret realize that sometimes Sylvia isn't any different from her other grandparents. Margaret wonders what difference religion even makes, anyway.

The next Friday, the sixth-graders must submit their individual year-long reports. Obviously, Margaret has come to no firm conclusions in the course of her religion experiment; instead of a report, she simply hands Mr. Benedict a letter explaining the situation, describing all the different churches and temples she visited and admitting that she didn't feel any attachment to any of them. She tries to tell him in person, but gets upset and begins to cry, so she runs away to the bathroom.

At the very end of the year, the PTA throws the class a farewell party; the sixth-graders give Mr. Benedict a gift and thank him, and in return he thanks them for giving him lots of experience so that he will go into his next year of teaching knowing exactly what he's doing. The four PTSes have their own lunch alone downtown and discuss what it will be like to go to Junior High, and Margaret's mother begins packing Margaret's trunk for camp that summer. When Margaret sees Moose outside mowing the lawn, she accuses him of lying about going behind the A&P with Laura Danker—Moose is shocked at the accusation, denies that he ever said anything, and tells Margaret that she shouldn't believe everything she hears. Margaret realizes that Moose is right.

Margaret is still thinking about Moose as she goes inside into the bathroom; suddenly, she looks down at her underpants and sees that she's actually gotten her period. She can't believe it and calls for her mom. Her mom is naturally excited for her, and tries to show her how to use pads; Margaret laughs and says she's been practicing in her room for two months. Later, Margaret talks to God again for the first time in a long time and thanks him for finally helping her to grow up.

# Analysis

The contrast between Margaret's maternal grandparents and her grandmother Sylvia is most prominent in these chapters. Where Sylvia is outspoken and doting, Margaret's mother's parents are colder and quieter, and their attempts to get to know Margaret seem forced and insincere. But there is one area, as Margaret acknowledges, in which they all are alike: they all think they know what's best for Margaret when it comes to religion. Sylvia, of course, has known Margaret her whole life, so she's grown used to the idea that Margaret will choose for herself, but she still drops hints and pressures Margaret now and again. In that way, she isn't too different from the other grandparents.

Now that we've reached the end of the novel, it is important to discuss the ways in which Margaret has grown or, as is the proper phrase for novels such as this one, "come of age." She has, of course, physically grown up since she first moved to Farbrook, New Jersey: she began to wear her first bra, developed her first crush, and got her period for the very first time. Most of the things she hoped would happen have happened over the course of the school year, and while she may not be as big or developed as girls like Laura Danker, she's reassured now that she is "normal" and growing correctly.

In terms of religion, Margaret has certainly reached a bit of a stalemate: she's experimented with churches and temples, with Christianity and Judaism, but she hasn't felt a connection strong enough to justify devoting her life to one or the other. This lack of progress upsets her, as evidenced by her breakdown when she tries to talk to Mr. Benedict about it, but in general, by the end of the novel she seems okay with the idea of maintaining her personal relationship with God. She would prefer to continue her own private discussions, rather than try to force a religious choice that she clearly isn't ready to make yet, if she even makes one at all. Margaret makes an important point when Sylvia comes to visit from Florida: as long as her grandma loves her and she loves her grandma, what difference does religion make?

But slowly, as she changes physically and explores her different religious options, Margaret changes in a few profound psychological ways as well. Over the course of her journey through the sixth grade, Margaret has learned many important lessons. For one, rumors can be vicious; she must not listen to everything she hears about someone. For another, plans can change, and disappointments may come—she must learn to go with the flow and accept conflicts as she encounters them. She's also learned that forgiveness is important; yes, Nancy lied to her about her period, but she had to forgive her because everyone makes mistakes. If Margaret hadn't forgiven, her friendship with Nancy would have remained in jeopardy.

Most importantly, though, Margaret learns that she must be patient in all aspects of life. When it comes to growing up, things don't move very quickly when you sit around waiting for them; however, if you are patient, time will fly by much more quickly than you might expect. Margaret has learned that waiting can be necessary:

waiting for her body to change, waiting for a boy to like her, and of course waiting to determine which religion is right for her. By the end of the novel, this young protagonist has realized that waiting produces rewards, and that it is important not to rush because without new milestones in the distance, there will be nothing to look forward to.

# Suggested Essay Questions

1. **Discuss how *Are You There God?* is a *bildungsroman*, or coming-of-age novel.**

   A *bildungsroman* tells the story of a young person growing into his or her own skin and discovering what it means to be mature, and *Are You There God?* details exactly this situation from the perspective of Margaret Simon. Readers watch as Margaret traverses her road to becoming a woman; she buys her first bra, has her first kiss, and gets her first period. But the most important changes involve Margaret's mindset. At the end of the novel, she accepts that the things she wants will come with time and patience, and understands that she cannot rush adulthood. This nuanced psychological angle is truly what a coming-of-age novel is about.

2. **What does Margaret ultimately decide about religion, and how does she come to this conclusion?**

   Throughout the novel, Margaret assumes that she needs to make a decision between Christianity and Judaism in order to fit in with everyone else. She tries going to church, to temple, and even to confession, but in none of these places does she feel the connection with God that everyone had talked about. Eventually, she decides that right now, religion does not have to be an important part of her life; she can't rush a decision as important as this one. The pressure both from her maternal grandparents and from Sylvia decides this for her; Margaret's quote "As long as she loves me and I love her, what difference does religion make?" sums this mentality up nicely.

3. **What influence do Margaret's three close friends have on her in the novel?**

   Because Margaret is new to town, she looks to Nancy, Gretchen, and Janie, her three new friends, to discover how she should behave and who she's supposed to be. Because of this, these friends play a profound role in shaping Margaret's identity throughout her sixth grade year. By far the most powerful influence is Nancy, who has a very commanding and informative role within Margaret's circle of closest comrades. Margaret begins listening to Nancy's advice immediately, when Nancy tells her not to wear socks with her loafers on the first day of school. Margaret very often feels the need to conform to what her friends are doing, but this tendency trickles away by the end of the novel as she begins to feel more comfortable in her own skin.

4. **How would this story be different if it were told from another character's point of view?**

   Undoubtedly, many key elements of this story would have been preserved had the story been told from the point of view of one of Margaret's peers, since they all are experiencing the new world of adolescence in roughly similar ways. However, Margaret's struggle with religion truly sets her apart from all the other sixth-graders; particularly during the time period when the novel is set (the 1970s), it wasn't common for a child to grow up without a religion, so this aspect of the story is unique to Margaret. It was important for Blume to add this extra dimension to make *Are You There God? It's Me, Margaret* more than just a typical novel about adolescence.

5. **How would Margaret's experiences be different if she were a young girl growing up in the present day? How would they be similar?**

The timelessness of this novel has kept it popular since its publication, since things like bras, boys, and periods are things adolescent girls worry about all the time, from generation to generation. Some things, however, would have been different if Margaret's story were set in present-day society; for one, she probably would not have had as much pressure to choose a religion as she did then. In our own time, more and more parents are choosing not to raise their children in a specific religion, and marriage between people of different religions occurs much more than it once did.

6. **Why is Laura Danker such an important character in this novel?**

Appearance-wise, Laura Danker is everything Margaret and the other girls want to be, but as a result, Laura is treated poorly. It was important for Bloom to include a character who illustrates the devastating results of jealousy, rumors, and simply being different, even in relatively small ways. Laura taught Margaret an important lesson: rumors are rarely true. Rather than let something she hears about someone influence her opinion of them, Margaret learns to get to know others first, without forming preconceptions. Laura is clearly not what everyone makes her out to be, but Margaret had never given her a chance.

7. **Because he is their teacher, the sixth grade children obviously learn a lot from Mr. Benedict. Conversely, what does *he* learn from *them*?**

Being a brand-new teacher can be daunting, but Mr. Benedict was clearly suited to the job. Though the sixth-graders tested him at first, he was quick to shut rebellion down and eventually gains their respect. Mr. Benedict learns a lot from his very first class of students, including when to be strict, when to be compassionate, and when to be a little of both. He learns that all of his students are different, and comes to know each of them better through their yearlong individual projects. Mr. Benedict is a prime example of the truth that a teacher can learn just as much from his students as they do from him.

8. **Was Sylvia truly too much of an influence on Margaret? Why or why not?**

Considering the authoritarian manner in which Mrs. Simon's parents reacted to their daughter marrying a Jewish man, it is understandable that Margaret's parents felt that, as Margaret got older, Sylvia would become too much of an influence. But in reality, Sylvia was an essential figure in Margaret's childhood; she provided not only care, but also the kind of friendship and support that an only child sometimes has difficulty receiving. While she sometimes made comments that pressured Margaret into choosing Judaism, Sylvia was never overbearing or forceful. Having at least one grandparent was important for a child like Margaret, and Sylvia filled that role wonderfully.

9. **Do you think it was right for Margaret to keep Nancy's secret? Why or why not?**

During her outing with Nancy in New York City, Margaret made a wise decision to push away her feelings of betrayal and instead be a good friend. It would have been easy for Margaret to let her emotions get away with her; after all, if Nancy had been lying about her period, what else could she have been lying about? But in forgiving Nancy and agreeing to keep her secret, Margaret made a very adult decision that ultimately paid off in the long run. A tiny deception is not worth losing a best friend over.

10. **Did Margaret's move from New York City to New Jersey help her or hinder her in the long run?**

Though shifting from urban to suburban life is undoubtedly a huge change, Margaret handled this transition gracefully, and ultimately emerged a better and more well-rounded person. As a private school student and an only child with an extremely doting grandmother, Margaret lived a sheltered life, and her physical move from one place to another also represents a symbolic shift: the beginning of Margaret's growth and maturity. Though the peer pressures she finds in her new town and at the public school are certainly overbearing at times, these forces teach Margaret many valuable lessons. Out in New Jersey, Margaret is better able to understand herself and to come to terms with what she wants from her family.

# Then Again, Maybe I Won't — A Male's Take on Adolesence

*Are You There God? It's Me, Margaret*, which details a girl's transition from puberty to womanhood, is one of Judy Blume's more famous works. Yet many readers are unaware that that this novel inspired a counterpart called *Then Again, Maybe I Won't*, which revolves around a boy's transition from puberty to manhood. Though this novel explores slightly different secondary themes, the primary theme of coming-of-age is still ever-present.

The protagonist of *Then Again, Maybe I Won't*, Tony Miglione, lives in a middle-class neighborhood in Jersey City, New Jersey, until his father acquires a large sum of wealth from one of his inventions; after that, the family moves to an upper-class community in Rosemont, New York. Things are different there, for obvious reasons, but Tony still manages to make a friend, Joel Hoober, who seems polite and polished but really has some rebellious tendencies. He encourages Tony to adopt his lifestyle of prank calls, drinking, and shoplifting.

A lot of other changes occur for Tony at roughly the same time. As a result of her new life, Tony's mother becomes hellbent on climbing the social ladder. Tony's older brother's wife has a new baby, and then gets pregnant once again. And Tony himself becomes infatuated with Joel's teenage sister Lisa, and gets to know a girl named Corky who appears to like him (even though he doesn't like her back). Finally, Tony is enrolled in therapy because of serious concerns about Joel's negative influence.

At last, Tony gets over Lisa when he finds out she has a boyfriend, and ends his friendship with Joel because of his thievery. Joel's father is planning to send Joel to a military academy, and Joel even reveals that all of his bad behavior was the result of his parents' neglect.

Some of the secondary themes in this novel are more adult-oriented than the side topics in *Are You There God?*, but both Margaret and Tony are fundamentally similar: they deal not only with growing up and experiencing puberty, but also with more nuanced problems such as exploring religion and succumbing to secretive activity. Since it was inspired by Margaret's story, *Then Again, Maybe I Won't* is a wonderful companion to this novel and an interesting look at the other side of the coming-of-age coin.

Then Again, Maybe I Won't — A Male's Take on Adolesence

# Author of ClassicNote and Sources

Kathryn Gundersen, author of ClassicNote. Completed on May 15, 2014, copyright held by GradeSaver.

Updated and revised Patrick Kennedy June 16, 2014. Copyright held by GradeSaver.

Judy Blume. Are You There God? It's Me, Margaret. New York, NY: Yearling, 1970.

Judy Blume. Are You There God? It's Me, Margaret Summary & Study Guide. Seattle, WA: BookRags, 2000.

Lev Grossman. "All Time 100 Novels." Time. 2005-10-16. 2014-04-20. <http://entertainment.time.com/2005/10/16/all-time-100-novels/>.

Mallory Szymanski. "Adolescence, Literature, and Censorship." NeoAmericanist. 2014-05-02. <http://www.neoamericanist.org/paper/adolescence-literature-and-censorship-unpacking-contr

# Quiz 1

1. **In what state was author Judy Blume raised?**
   A. New York
   B. Massachusetts
   C. Delaware
   D. New Jersey

2. **Which two universities did author Judy Blume attend?**
   A. Boston University and New York University
   B. St. John's University and Columbia University
   C. Rutgers University and Princeton University
   D. Cornell University and Duke University

3. **Judy Blume obtained a bachelor's degree in which area?**
   A. English
   B. Teaching
   C. Creative Writing
   D. Comparative Literature

4. **What was the title of Blume's first published book?**
   A. I[The One in the Middle is the Green Kangaroo]
   B. I[Then Again, Maybe I Won't]
   C. I[Tales of a Fourth Grade Nothing]
   D. I[Are You There God? It's Me, Margaret]

5. **In what year was I[Are You There God?] published?**
   A. 1962
   B. 1970
   C. 1987
   D. 2000

6. **Which Judy Blume novel tells a story similar to Margaret's, but from a male perspective?**
   A. I[Then Again, Maybe I Won't]
   B. I[Blubber]
   C. I[Tales of a Fourth Grade Nothing]
   D. I[Superfudge]

7. **Where did Margaret and her family originally live?**
    A. Philadelphia
    B. Boston
    C. Jersey City
    D. New York City

8. **Where do Margaret and her family move to?**
    A. Westchester, New York
    B. New Haven, Connecticut
    C. Massapequa, Long Island
    D. Farbrook, New Jersey

9. **Why does Margaret believe her parents wanted to move?**
    A. Mrs. Simon's parents asked them to move out of the city.
    B. Margaret's parents thought that the city was too dangerous.
    C. They were worried that Margaret's grandmother was too much of an influence on her.
    D. They couldn't afford their New York apartment anymore.

10. **What is Margaret's mother's name?**
    A. Sylvia
    B. Barbara
    C. Jane
    D. Nancy

11. **What is Margaret's father's name?**
    A. Harold
    B. Philip
    C. Herb
    D. Bill

12. **What is Margaret's paternal grandmother's name?**
    A. Sylvia
    B. Gretchen
    C. Lucy
    D. Laura

13. **What grade year will Margaret be entering in school?**
    A. Seventh grade
    B. Fifth grade
    C. Sixth grade
    D. Fourth grade

14. **Who is Margaret's very first friend in her new town?**
    A. Nancy Wheeler
    B. Gretchen Potter
    C. Laura Danker
    D. Janie Loomis

15. **What is Nancy like?**
    A. Very friendly, but something of a know-it-all.
    B. Rude, blunt, and extremely rebellious.
    C. Quiet, shy, and nurturing.
    D. Reserved and distrustful.

16. **What is the name of the neighborhood boy whom Margaret develops a crush on?**
    A. Leo
    B. Jay
    C. Hawk
    D. Moose

17. **What type of handiwork does Moose Freed offer to do for the Simons?**
    A. Watering the flowers
    B. Building a shed
    C. Mowing the lawn
    D. Paving the sidewalk

18. **What religion was Margaret's father brought up in?**
    A. Christianity
    B. Judaism
    C. Buddhism
    D. Islam

19. **What religion was Margaret's mother brought up in?**
    A. Christianity
    B. Judaism
    C. Buddhism
    D. Islam

20. **Why did Mrs. Simon's parents reject their daughter and refuse to speak to her?**
    A. She became pregnant out of wedlock.
    B. She was arrested for drunk driving.
    C. She married a Jewish man.
    D. She wanted to pursue a career they didn't approve of.

21. **What does Nancy tell Margaret not to do on the first day of school?**
    A. Wear socks with her loafers.
    B. Wear a ponytail.
    C. Bring a lunch from home.
    D. Act like she's the new girl.

22. **What is the name of the sixth grade's new teacher?**
    A. Mr. Birmingham
    B. Mr. Barnes
    C. Mr. Barnaby
    D. Mr. Benedict

23. **What type of project does Mr. Benedict ask his class to complete?**
    A. An interview-based study of the behavior of those around them
    B. A book report on a novel from another time period
    C. An individual contribution to the mural being painted in the school hallway
    D. A year-long individual project exploring a topic of personal importance

24. **What is the name of the sixth-grade girl who is bigger and more developed than any of the others?**
    A. Lauren
    B. Lisa
    C. Laila
    D. Laura

25. **Aside from Margaret and Nancy, who are the two other girls in the secret club?**
    A. Laura Danker and Norma Fishbein
    B. Kristen Leroy and Tina Thompson
    C. Gretchen Potter and Janie Loomis
    D. Jenna Hassler and Barbara Benedict

# Quiz 1 Answer Key

1. **(D)** New Jersey
2. **(A)** Boston University and New York University
3. **(B)** Teaching
4. **(A)** I[The One in the Middle is the Green Kangaroo]
5. **(B)** 1970
6. **(A)** I[Then Again, Maybe I Won't]
7. **(D)** New York City
8. **(D)** Farbrook, New Jersey
9. **(C)** They were worried that Margaret's grandmother was too much of an influence on her.
10. **(B)** Barbara
11. **(C)** Herb
12. **(A)** Sylvia
13. **(C)** Sixth grade
14. **(A)** Nancy Wheeler
15. **(A)** Very friendly, but something of a know-it-all.
16. **(D)** Moose
17. **(C)** Mowing the lawn
18. **(B)** Judaism
19. **(A)** Christianity
20. **(C)** She married a Jewish man.
21. **(A)** Wear socks with her loafers.
22. **(D)** Mr. Benedict
23. **(D)** A year-long individual project exploring a topic of personal importance
24. **(D)** Laura
25. **(C)** Gretchen Potter and Janie Loomis

# Quiz 2

1. **What do the girls decide to name their club?**
   A. Sixth Grade Cu-Tees (SGCT)
   B. Glamour Girls (GG)
   C. Pre-Teen Sensations (PTS)
   D. Miles J. Benedict Girls (MJB Girls)

2. **What are the girls' four secret club code names?**
   A. Kimberly, Veronica, Alexandra, Mavis
   B. Spring, Summer, Autumn, Winter
   C. Portia, Tiffany, Nicole, Olivia
   D. Rose, Lily, Pansy, Violet

3. **Which of the secret club names is Margaret given?**
   A. Veronica
   B. Kimberly
   C. Alexandra
   D. Mavis

4. **Which rule does Margaret propose for the club?**
   A. They tell each other when they get their periods
   B. They make Boy Books
   C. They meet one day each week
   D. They buy bras

5. **What does Margaret need to do before the second PTS meeting?**
   A. Buy a bra
   B. Kiss a boy
   C. Tease Mr. Benedict
   D. Buy menstrual pads

6. **Which friend does Margaret run into while shopping for her first bra?**
   A. Gretchen
   B. Janie
   C. Laura
   D. Nancy

7. **Who is ranked first in all the PTS Boy Books?**
    A. Norman Fishbein
    B. Mr. Benedict
    C. Jay Hassler
    D. Philip Leroy

8. **What is the first way the students give Mr. Benedict trouble?**
    A. They move all the desks out of the room
    B. They make peeping noises throughout the classroom
    C. They are all absent from school on the same day
    D. They draw pictures of animals all over the blackboard

9. **What is the second way that the students tease Mr. Benedict?**
    A. They bring mice into the classroom
    B. They agree not to put their names on their Social Studies tests
    C. They all move seats before he enters the room
    D. They pretend not to hear him every time he talks

10. **What subject does Margaret decide to explore for her year-long project?**
    A. New Jersey's history
    B. Different cities around the world
    C. Her choice of religion
    D. Growing up

11. **What rumor do the other students spread about Laura Danker?**
    A. She secretly stuffs her bra.
    B. She goes behind the A&P with older boys.
    C. She is going to fail out of sixth grade.
    D. She still hasn't gotten her period yet.

12. **Where do Margaret and Sylvia go on one weekend of every month?**
    A. The Statue of Liberty
    B. Lincoln Center
    C. On a circle-line cruise
    D. The New Jersey Shore

13. **On what Jewish holiday does Margaret visit temple with Sylvia?**
    A. Rosh Hashannah
    B. Hanukkah
    C. Passover
    D. Yom Kippur

14. **How does Margaret pass the time in temple?**
    A. She counts colorful hats
    B. She whispers to her grandmother
    C. She talks to God in her mind
    D. She sings songs in her head

15. **With which friend does Margaret go to church for the first time?**
    A. Gretchen
    B. Janie
    C. Laura
    D. Nancy

16. **What type of dance does the PTA hold for the class?**
    A. A square dance
    B. A costume ball
    C. A salsa contest
    D. A New Year's dance

17. **Whom do all the PTSes want to dance with at the class dance?**
    A. Norman Fishbein
    B. Mr. Benedict
    C. Jay Hassler
    D. Philip Leroy

18. **Whom does Mr. Benedict use as his partner in a demonstration of dance techniques?**
    A. Gretchen
    B. Margaret
    C. Laura
    D. Nancy

### 19. Why does Margaret keep Philip at the top of her Boy Book?

A. He told her he likes her.

B. He's handsome, and she's afraid to admit who she really likes.

C. She and Janie have an agreement that they always will.

D. Nancy forces her to.

### 20. Whom does Margaret really have a crush on?

A. Norman Fishbein

B. Moose Freed

C. Jay Hassler

D. Evan Wheeler

### 21. Which of her father's magazines does Margaret steal?

A. I[People]

B. I[Sports Illustrated]

C. I[Playboy]

D. I[Time]

### 22. Who receives a surprise holiday card from Margaret's mother?

A. Sylvia

B. Margaret's maternal grandparents

C. Mr. Benedict

D. Laura Danker

### 23. What kind of vacation does Sylvia take in December?

A. An adventure to Europe

B. A ski trip

C. A Caribbean cruise

D. A hiking trip

### 24. Who is Margaret's partner for the Christmas-Hannukah pageant?

A. Freddy Barnett

B. Norman Fishbein

C. Jay Hassler

D. Philip Leroy

25. **Which two PTS club traditions are abandoned by December?**
    A. Monday Meetings and Boy Books
    B. Boy Books and Code Names
    C. Monday Meetings and Bras
    D. Code Names and Bras

# Quiz 2 Answer Key

1. **(C)** Pre-Teen Sensations (PTS)
2. **(A)** Kimberly, Veronica, Alexandra, Mavis
3. **(D)** Mavis
4. **(C)** They meet one day each week
5. **(A)** Buy a bra
6. **(B)** Janie
7. **(D)** Philip Leroy
8. **(B)** They make peeping noises throughout the classroom
9. **(B)** They agree not to put their names on their Social Studies tests
10. **(C)** Her choice of religion
11. **(B)** She goes behind the A&P with older boys.
12. **(B)** Lincoln Center
13. **(A)** Rosh Hashannah
14. **(A)** She counts colorful hats
15. **(B)** Janie
16. **(A)** A square dance
17. **(D)** Philip Leroy
18. **(C)** Laura
19. **(B)** He's handsome, and she's afraid to admit who she really likes.
20. **(B)** Moose Freed
21. **(C)** I[Playboy]
22. **(B)** Margaret's maternal grandparents
23. **(C)** A Caribbean cruise
24. **(B)** Norman Fishbein
25. **(B)** Boy Books and Code Names

# Quiz 3

1. **What is the chant that the PTSes use to grow their chests?**
   A. "A pinch to grow an inch!"
   B. "We'd like to rise a size!"
   C. "Grow bigger grow bigger grow bigger!"
   D. "We must increase our bust!"

2. **Which student in the class throws a dinner party?**
   A. Nancy Wheeler
   B. Norman Fishbein
   C. Laura Danker
   D. Philip Leroy

3. **What does Margaret do to change her appearance before she goes to the dinner party?**
   A. She puts on new makeup.
   B. She stuffs her bra with cotton balls.
   C. She shaves her arms.
   D. She gives herself an impromptu haircut.

4. **At the dinner party, which two students get in a fight that results in a ripped dress?**
   A. Gretchen and Jay
   B. Freddy and Nancy
   C. Norman and Laura
   D. Margaret and Philip

5. **What do the boys do to misbehave at the party?**
   A. Make fun of Mrs. Fishbein.
   B. Blow mustard at the ceiling through straws.
   C. Throw food at each other.
   D. Unclasp the girls' bras when they aren't looking.

6. **What is the first party game that the sixth-graders play?**
   A. Spin the Bottle
   B. Guess Who
   C. Pin the Tail on the Donkey
   D. Two Minutes in the Closet

7. **Which girl does Philip Leroy have to kiss during spin the bottle?**
    A. Margaret
    B. Janie
    C. Laura
    D. Nancy

8. **What is the second party game that the sixth-graders play?**
    A. Guess Who
    B. Pin the Tail on the Donkey
    C. Two Minutes in the Closet
    D. Limbo

9. **Who kisses Margaret on the mouth during Two Minutes in the Closet?**
    A. Freddy Barnett
    B. Norman Fishbein
    C. Jay Hassler
    D. Philip Leroy

10. **Who is the second boy who goes into the closet with Margaret?**
    A. Freddy Barnett
    B. Norman Fishbein
    C. Jay Hassler
    D. Philip Leroy

11. **Which friend does Margaret accompany to church on Christmas Eve?**
    A. Philip
    B. Gretchen
    C. Janie
    D. Nancy

12. **Where does Sylvia move immediately after she returns from her cruise?**
    A. Florida
    B. New Jersey
    C. Louisiana
    D. California

### 13. Which of the PTSes gets her period first?
A. Gretchen
B. Margaret
C. Janie
D. Nancy

### 14. Which brand of menstrual supplies do Gretchen and all the other PTSes decide to use?
A. Tampax
B. Always
C. Teenage Softies
D. Private Lady

### 15. How does Nancy tell Margaret she got her period?
A. She sends her a postcard while on vacation.
B. She calls her on the phone.
C. She passes Margaret a note.
D. She announces it at recess.

### 16. Who is Sylvia's new beau?
A. Mr. Birmingham
B. Mr. Binamin
C. Mr. Bartley
D. Mr. Cinnamon

### 17. Sylvia invites Margaret to visit Florida during which school vacation?
A. Spring vacation
B. Summer vacation
C. Thanksgiving vacation
D. Winter vacation

### 18. Where does Margaret go with the Wheelers and Moose to spend the day?
A. Philadelphia
B. Long Island
C. The New Jersey Shore
D. New York City

19. **Where do Margaret and Nancy go during their trip to New York?**
    A. Radio City Music Hall
    B. The Statue of Liberty
    C. Lincoln Center
    D. The Empire State Building

20. **What does Margaret learn about Nancy in New York?**
    A. Nancy is failing Mr. Benedict's class.
    B. Nancy is secretly in love with Moose.
    C. Nancy had lied about her bra size.
    D. Nancy had lied about getting her period.

21. **How does Margaret react to learning the truth about Nancy?**
    A. She admits to Nancy that she had lied about something, too.
    B. She doesn't know what to think, and begins to cry.
    C. She's livid and tells the other PTSes right away.
    D. She feels betrayed, but she keeps Nancy's secret.

22. **When is Margaret's birthday?**
    A. March 8th
    B. April 21st
    C. February 13th
    D. May 2nd

23. **How old does Margaret turn in the book?**
    A. 9
    B. 11
    C. 12
    D. 13

24. **What does Margaret decide to start wearing on her birthday?**
    A. Makeup
    B. Socks with her loafers
    C. Deodorant
    D. A larger bra

25. **What does Sylvia send Margaret for her birthday?**
    A. A beautiful stone necklace and a golden bracelet
    B. A new pair of loafers and a new velvet dress
    C. A savings bond, three handmade sweaters, and a plane ticket
    D. A plane ticket and a gift certificate to Lincoln Center

# Quiz 3 Answer Key

1. **(D)** "We must increase our bust!"
2. **(B)** Norman Fishbein
3. **(B)** She stuffs her bra with cotton balls.
4. **(B)** Freddy and Nancy
5. **(B)** Blow mustard at the ceiling through straws.
6. **(A)** Spin the Bottle
7. **(C)** Laura
8. **(C)** Two Minutes in the Closet
9. **(D)** Philip Leroy
10. **(B)** Norman Fishbein
11. **(D)** Nancy
12. **(A)** Florida
13. **(A)** Gretchen
14. **(C)** Teenage Softies
15. **(A)** She sends her a postcard while on vacation.
16. **(B)** Mr. Binamin
17. **(A)** Spring vacation
18. **(D)** New York City
19. **(A)** Radio City Music Hall
20. **(D)** Nancy had lied about getting her period.
21. **(D)** She feels betrayed, but she keeps Nancy's secret.
22. **(A)** March 8th
23. **(C)** 12
24. **(C)** Deodorant
25. **(C)** A savings bond, three handmade sweaters, and a plane ticket

# Quiz 4

1. **The PTSes pool their money and buy what for Margaret as a birthday gift?**
   A. A gourmet cake
   B. A record
   C. Teenage Softies
   D. New shoes

2. **Whom does Margaret work with on a group project for school?**
   A. Gretchen, Freddy, Philip
   B. Laura, Philip, and Norman
   C. Gretchen, Janie, and Nancy
   D. Laura, Jay, and Janie

3. **Which country does Margaret's group decide to do the project on?**
   A. England
   B. Belgium
   C. Austria
   D. France

4. **Laura leaves the library after working on the project early in order to go where?**
   A. Temple
   B. The A&P
   C. Confession
   D. New York City

5. **What does Laura do when Margaret accuses her of going behind the A&P with boys?**
   A. She says she does something else instead
   B. She falls to the ground and begins to cry
   C. She denies it and grows extremely angry
   D. She admits it

6. **Why does Laura think everyone picks on her?**
   A. She's too quiet
   B. She's ugly
   C. She is bigger than everyone else
   D. She picks on everyone else

7. **What does Margaret say at Confession?**
   A. "I don't have a religion"
   B. "I'm sorry"
   C. "Are you God?"
   D. "I made fun of Laura"

8. **Just before spring break, the Simons receive a letter sent by...**
   A. Sylvia
   B. Margaret's maternal grandparents
   C. Mr. Binamin
   D. Mr. Benedict

9. **What does the letter from Margaret's maternal grandparents say?**
   A. They want the Simons to visit them.
   B. They're moving to New Jersey.
   C. They ripped up the holiday card and still refuse to speak to their daughter.
   D. They would like to meet Margaret, so they're coming to visit over spring break.

10. **Margaret is upset because her maternal grandparents interfere with which of her plans?**
    A. Staying at a lake with Nancy
    B. Catching up on her group project
    C. Visiting Sylvia in Florida
    D. Spending a weekend in New York City

11. **What is the first thing Margaret notices about her maternal grandmother at the airport?**
    A. She's wearing all black.
    B. She's wearing a huge cross.
    C. She uses a gigantic metal walker.
    D. She's the tallest person Margaret has ever seen.

12. **What topic do Margaret's maternal grandparents raise during dinner?**
    A. Margaret getting her period.
    B. Margaret's other grandma.
    C. Margaret going to public school.
    D. Margaret's religion.

13. **What religion do Margaret's maternal grandparents think Margaret should be?**
    A. Jewish
    B. Muslim
    C. Buddhist
    D. Christian

14. **Why do Margaret's maternal grandparents believe that Margaret is meant to be Christian?**
    A. Margaret looks like one of the Christian saints.
    B. God has sent a sign.
    C. Margaret will only go to heaven if she chooses Christianity.
    D. Margaret's mother was a Christian.

15. **How does Margaret react to her maternal grandparents' efforts to convert her?**
    A. She screams that she's already chosen to be Jewish.
    B. She immediately calls Sylvia.
    C. She storms off upstairs and denies that she needs religion or God at all.
    D. She puts her head on the table and begins to cry.

16. **Where do Janie and Margaret stop while on their way to a movie downtown?**
    A. The drug store
    B. The candy store
    C. The school
    D. The pet store

17. **What do they buy there?**
    A. Menstrual pads
    B. School supplies
    C. Bras
    D. I[Playboy] magazine

18. **What do Margaret's maternal grandparents announce?**
    A. They want to take Margaret back to Ohio with them.
    B. They want Margaret's parents get divorced.
    C. They're sorry for what they said and they want to apologize to Margaret.
    D. They'll be leaving the house early and are going to stay in New York instead.

19. **Who shows up on Margaret's doorstep right after Margaret's maternal grandparents leave?**
    A. Sylvia and Mr. Binamin
    B. Janie, Gretchen, and Nancy
    C. Mr. Benedict
    D. Mrs. Wheeler

20. **What does Margaret submit instead of a report for her year-long project?**
    A. She doesn't submit anything
    B. A letter explaining that she couldn't choose a religion
    C. A summary of why she prefers Christianity
    D. A summary of why she prefers Judaism

21. **What do the students give Mr. Benedict as an end-of-the-year gift?**
    A. A camera
    B. Cuff links
    C. A tie
    D. A book

22. **Where will Margaret be going in the summer?**
    A. Camp in New Hampshire
    B. Nowhere, because she's staying at home
    C. To stay with Sylvia
    D. New York City

23. **What important advice does Moose give Margaret?**
    A. She shouldn't believe everything she hears.
    B. She needs to be patient, and good things will happen.
    C. Her bust exercises don't really work, and she should try something else.
    D. She doesn't have to choose a religion yet.

24. **Just after talking to Moose, what happens to Margaret?**
    A. She can no longer fit into her bra.
    B. She gets her period.
    C. She discovers that she needs deodorant.
    D. She realizes that she doesn't have a crush on Moose any longer.

25. **What happens at the end of the novel?**
    A. Margaret talks to Mr. Benedict.
    B. Margaret reconciles with God and thanks him for her period.
    C. The PTSes disband for good.
    D. Margaret's family moves back to New York.

# Quiz 4 Answer Key

1. **(B)** A record
2. **(B)** Laura, Philip, and Norman
3. **(B)** Belgium
4. **(C)** Confession
5. **(C)** She denies it and grows extremely angry
6. **(C)** She is bigger than everyone else
7. **(B)** "I'm sorry"
8. **(B)** Margaret's maternal grandparents
9. **(D)** They would like to meet Margaret, so they're coming to visit over spring break.
10. **(C)** Visiting Sylvia in Florida
11. **(B)** She's wearing a huge cross.
12. **(D)** Margaret's religion.
13. **(D)** Christian
14. **(D)** Margaret's mother was a Christian.
15. **(C)** She storms off upstairs and denies that she needs religion or God at all.
16. **(A)** The drug store
17. **(A)** Menstrual pads
18. **(D)** They'll be leaving the house early and are going to stay in New York instead.
19. **(A)** Sylvia and Mr. Binamin
20. **(B)** A letter explaining that she couldn't choose a religion
21. **(B)** Cuff links
22. **(A)** Camp in New Hampshire
23. **(A)** She shouldn't believe everything she hears.
24. **(B)** She gets her period.
25. **(B)** Margaret reconciles with God and thanks him for her period.

# ClassicNotes

# GrAdeSaver™

*Getting you the grade since 1999*™

## Other ClassicNotes from GradeSaver™

Catch-22
The Catcher in the Rye
Catching Fire
Cathedral
The Caucasian Chalk
    Circle
Charlotte Temple
Charlotte's Web
The Cherry Orchard
Chinese Cinderella
The Chocolate War
The Chosen
Christina Rossetti:
    Poems
A Christmas Carol
Christopher Marlowe's
    Poems
Chronicle of a Death
    Foretold
Citizen Kane
Civil Disobedience
Civil Peace
Civilization and Its
    Discontents
A Clockwork Orange
    (Film)
A Clockwork Orange
Cloud Atlas
Coleridge's Poems
The Collector
The Color of Water
The Color Purple
Comedy of Errors
Communist Manifesto
A Confederacy of
    Dunces

Confessions
Confessions of an
    English Opium Eater
Connecticut Yankee in
    King Arthur's Court
The Consolation of
    Philosophy
Coriolanus
The Count of Monte
    Cristo
The Country of the
    Pointed Firs and
    Other Stories
The Country Wife
Crime and Punishment
The Crucible
Cry, the Beloved
    Country
The Crying of Lot 49
The Curious Incident of
    the Dog in the
    Night-time
Cymbeline
Daisy Miller
David Copperfield
Death in Venice
Death of a Salesman
The Death of Ivan Ilych
Democracy in America
Devil in a Blue Dress
The Devil's Arithmetic
Dharma Bums
The Diary of a Young
    Girl by Anne Frank
Disgrace
Divergent

Divine Comedy-I:
    Inferno
Do Androids Dream of
    Electric Sheep?
Doctor Faustus
    (Marlowe)
A Doll's House
Don Quixote Book I
Don Quixote Book II
John Donne: Poems
Dora: An Analysis of a
    Case of Hysteria
Dr. Jekyll and Mr. Hyde
Dracula
Dubliners
The Duchess of Malfi
East of Eden
Edgar Huntly: Memoirs
    of a Sleep-Walker
Electra by Sophocles
The Electric Kool-Aid
    Acid Test
Emily Dickinson's
    Collected Poems
Emma
Ender's Game
Endgame
Enduring Love
The English Patient
Enrique's Journey
The Epic of Gilgamesh
Esperanza Rising
Eternal Sunshine of the
    Spotless Mind
Ethan Frome
The Eumenides

For our full list of over 250 Study Guides, Quizzes,
Sample College Application Essays, Literature Essays and E-texts, visit:

**www.gradesaver.com**

# ClassicNotes

# GrAdeSaver™

## *Getting you the grade since 1999*™

## Other ClassicNotes from GradeSaver™

Evelina
Everyman: Morality Play
Everything is Illuminated
Exeter Book
Extremely Loud and
    Incredibly Close
Ezra Pound: Poems
The Faerie Queene
Fahrenheit 451
The Fall of the House of
    Usher
A Farewell to Arms
The Federalist Papers
Fences
Fifth Business
Fight Club
Fight Club (Film)
Flags of Our Fathers
Flannery O'Connor's
    Stories
Flight
For Colored Girls Who
    Have Considered
    Suicide When the
    Rainbow Is Enuf
For Whom the Bell Tolls
Founding Brothers
The Fountainhead
Frankenstein
Franny and Zooey
Friday Night Lights
The Giver
The Glass Castle
The Glass Menagerie
The God of Small Things
The Godfather

Goethe's Faust
The Good Earth
The Good Woman of
    Setzuan
Gorilla, My Love
The Grapes of Wrath
Great Expectations
The Great Gatsby
Grendel
The Guest
Gulliver's Travels
Hamlet
The Handmaid's Tale
Hard Times
Haroun and the Sea of
    Stories
Harry Potter and the
    Philosopher's Stone
Heart of Darkness
The Heart of the Matter
Hedda Gabler
Henry IV (Pirandello)
Henry IV Part 1
Henry IV Part 2
Henry V
Herzog
Hippolytus
The History of Tom
    Jones, a Foundling
The Hobbit
Homo Faber
The Hot Zone
The Hound of the
    Baskervilles
The House of Bernarda
    Alba

House of Mirth
The House of the Seven
    Gables
The House of the Spirits
House on Mango Street
How the Garcia Girls
    Lost Their Accents
Howards End
A Hunger Artist
The Hunger Games
I Know Why the Caged
    Bird Sings
I, Claudius
An Ideal Husband
Iliad
The Importance of Being
    Earnest
In Cold Blood
In Our Time
In the Skin of a Lion
In the Time of the
    Butterflies
Incidents in the Life of a
    Slave Girl
Inherit the Wind
An Inspector Calls
Interpreter of Maladies
Into the Wild
Invisible Man
Ishmael
The Island of Dr. Moreau
Island of the Blue
    Dolphins
James and the Giant
    Peach
Jane Eyre

For our full list of over 250 Study Guides, Quizzes,
Sample College Application Essays, Literature Essays and E-texts, visit:

**www.gradesaver.com**

# ClassicNotes

# GradeSaver™

*Getting you the grade since 1999*™

## Other ClassicNotes from GradeSaver™

Moby Dick
Mockingjay
A Modest Proposal and Other Satires
Moll Flanders
The Most Dangerous Game
Mother Courage and Her Children
Mrs. Dalloway
Much Ado About Nothing
Murder in the Cathedral
My Antonia
Mythology
The Namesake
The Narrative of Arthur Gordon Pym of Nantucket
Narrative of the Life of Frederick Douglass
Native Son
Nervous Conditions
Never Let Me Go
New Introductory Lectures on Psychoanalysis
Nickel and Dimed: On (Not) Getting By in America
Night
Nine Stories
No Exit
North and South
Northanger Abbey
Notes from Underground

Number the Stars
O Pioneers
The Odyssey
Oedipus Rex or Oedipus the King
Of Mice and Men
The Old Man and the Sea
Oliver Twist
On Liberty
On the Road
One Day in the Life of Ivan Denisovich
One Flew Over the Cuckoo's Nest
One Hundred Years of Solitude
Oroonoko
Oryx and Crake
Othello
Our Town
The Outsiders
Pale Fire
Pamela: Or Virtue Rewarded
Paradise Lost
A Passage to India
The Pearl
Pedro Paramo
Percy Shelley: Poems
Perfume: The Story of a Murderer
The Perks of Being a Wallflower
Persepolis: The Story of a Childhood
Persuasion

Phaedra
Phaedrus
The Piano Lesson
The Picture of Dorian Gray
Pilgrim's Progress
The Playboy of the Western World
Poe's Poetry
Poe's Short Stories
Poems of W.B. Yeats: The Rose
Poems of W.B. Yeats: The Tower
The Poems of William Blake
The Poisonwood Bible
Pope's Poems and Prose
Portrait of the Artist as a Young Man
The Praise of Folly
Pride and Prejudice
The Prince
The Professor's House
Prometheus Bound
Pudd'nhead Wilson
Purple Hibiscus
Pygmalion
Rabbit, Run
A Raisin in the Sun
The Real Life of Sebastian Knight
Rebecca
The Red Badge of Courage
The Remains of the Day

For our full list of over 250 Study Guides, Quizzes,
Sample College Application Essays, Literature Essays and E-texts, visit:

**www.gradesaver.com**

Made in the USA
Las Vegas, NV
06 May 2023